A Gift
of Friendship...

To: _____

From: _____

Date: _____

*A friend is...
a whole lot of wonderful people
rolled into one.*

—Gayle Lawrence

Selected by Patricia Dreier
Artwork by Shelley Hely, courtesy of Art In Motion
Designed by Gail Smith

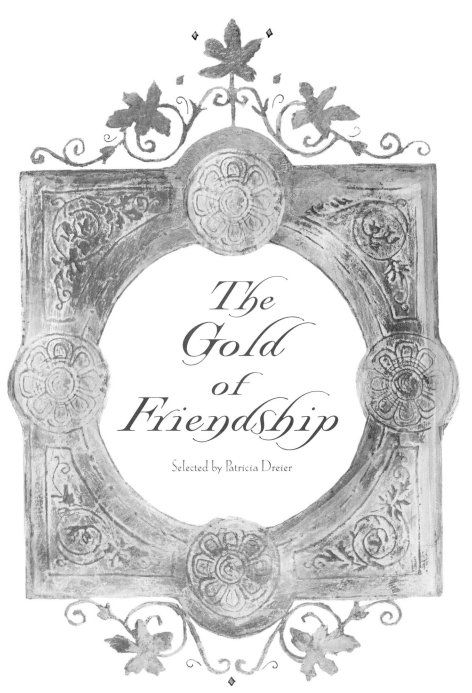

The Gold of Friendship

Selected by Patricia Dreier

C.R.Gibson® • Norwalk, Connecticut U.S.A.

Tulipa aurei coloris

Tulipa aurei coloris

Tulipa

Tulipa aurei coloris

Tulipa aurei coloris

Tulipa

I.V.

Friendship Is...

It is a sweet thing, friendship, a dear balm,
A happy and auspicious bird of calm,
Which rides o'er life's ever tumultuous Ocean;
A God that broods o'er chaos in commotion;
A flower which fresh as Lapland roses are,
Lifts its bold head into the world's frore air,
And blooms most radiantly when others die,
Health, hope, and youth, and brief prosperity;
And with the light and odour of its bloom,
Shining within the dungeon and the tomb;
Whose coming is as light and music are
'Mid dissonance and gloom a star
Which moves not 'mid the moving heavens alone—
A smile among dark frowns a gentle tone
Among rude voices, a beloved light,
A solitude, a refuge, a delight.

Percy Bysshe Shelley

Human Need

Courage we need for this life of ours,
Courage, calmness, power;
Glee in the present which children own,
Hope for the coming hour.

Underneath, and all the time,
A warm pulse, beating
To Nature's beauty, loved one's rhythm
The springtime urge repeating.

What will give us courage deep,
Joy in the things that are?
The true and lasting love of friends
For us, will go most far.

Madeline Benedict

Friendship

Friendship needs no studied phrases,
Polished face, or winning wiles;
Friendship deals no lavish praises,
Friendship dons no surface smiles.
Friendship follows Nature's diction,
Shuns the blandishments of Art,
Boldly severs truth from fiction,
Speaks the language of the heart.
Friendship—pure, unselfish friendship,
All through life's allotted span,
Nurtures, strengthens, widens, lengthens,
Man's relationship with man.

Author Unknown

Everyone Needs Friends

Without friends no one would choose to live, though he had all other goods; even rich men and those in possession of office and of dominating power are thought to need friends most of all; for what is the use of such prosperity without the opportunity of beneficence, which is exercised chiefly and in its most laudable form toward friends? Or how can prosperity be guarded and preserved without friends? The greater it is, the more exposed is it to risk. And in poverty and in other misfortunes men think friends are the only refuge. It helps the young, too, to keep from error; it aids older people by ministering to their needs and supplementing the activities that are failing from weakness; those in the prime of life it stimulates to noble actions... for with friends men are more able both to think and to act.

Aristotle

She Is My Friend

She listens when I talk, but more than that, she always hears me. She hears the subtle shading in my voice that tells her what my words do not. She catches feelings, carefully concealed behind the words, and understands.

She is my friend, and so she doesn't damage my hurt pride by pointing out my frailties. She simply says a thoughtful word or two, and suddenly I'm able to accept, to speak aloud my worries and embarrassments. I talk to her, and, as I do, my confidence returns.

Her friendship once again has shored me up, and I can face my fears and laugh them down. How many times she's listened when I talk, and how I count on her to really hear me.

Raphael Marie Turnbull

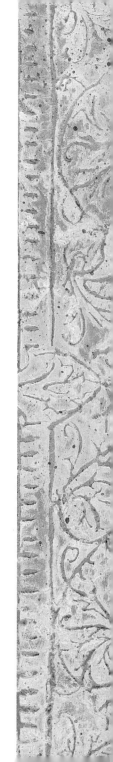

The Wealth of Friendship

There is no treasure which may be compared unto a
       faithful friend;
Gold soon decayeth and worldly wealth consumeth,
       and wasteth in the wind;
But love once planted in a perfect and pure mind
       endureth weal and woe;
The frowns of fortune, come they never so unkind,
       cannot it overthrow.

Author Unknown

The Things I Prize

These are the things I prize
And hold of dearest worth:
Light of the sapphire skies,
Peace of the silent hills,
Shelter of the forests, comfort of the grass,
Music of birds, murmur of little rills,
Shadows of clouds that swiftly pass,
And, after showers,
The smell of flowers
And of the good brown earth—
And best of all, along the way, friendship and mirth.

Henry Van Dyke

Friends Are Like Flowers

Friends are like flowers. I have found them so:
The hardy staunch perennials that grow
Year after year are like some friends I know.

One need not cultivate them with great care,
They only need the sun and wind and air
Of trust and love, and they are always there.

Some must be nursed with frequent trowel and spade,
And sheltered from the sun, or too much shade,
For fear their frail and clinging bloom may fade.

Friends are like flowers, I would be a friend
Whose blossomings no hand need ever tend:
A perennial on whom hearts can depend.

Grace Noll Crowell

I Want a Friend

I want a warm and faithful friend,
To cheer the adverse hour;
Who ne'er to flatter will descend,
Nor bend the knee to power;
A friend to chide me when I'm wrong,
My inmost soul to see;
And that my friendship prove as strong
To him as his to me.

John Quincy Adams

What We Need

"A friend in need," my neighbor said to me—
"A friend in deed is what I mean to be;
In time of trouble I will come to you
And in the hour of need you'll find me true."

I thought a bit, and took him by the hand,
"My friend," I said, "you do not understand
The inner meaning of that simple rhyme—
A friend is what the heart needs all the time."

Author Unknown

A Friend Listens

I have noted that the best and closest friends
are those who seldom call on each other for
help. In fact, such is almost the finest
definition of a friend—a person who does not
need us but who is able to enjoy us.

I have seldom suffered over the troubles of a friend. Are his
mishaps short of tragedy, I am inclined to chuckle. And he is
seldom serious in telling me of his misfortunes. He makes
anecdotes out of them, postures comically in their midst and tries to
entertain me with them. This is one of the chief values of my
friendship, as it is of his. We enable each other to play the strong
man superior to his fate. Given a friend to listen, my own disasters
change color. I win victories while relating them. Not only have I
a friend on my side who will believe my version of the battle— and
permit me to seem a victor in my communiques— but I have actually
a victory in me. I am able to show my friend my untouched side.
My secret superiority to bad events becomes stronger when I can
speak and have a friend believe in it.

Ben Hecht

Begin The Day

Begin the day with friendliness and only friends you'll find...
Yes, greet the dawn with happiness, keep happy thoughts in
mind...Salute the day with peaceful thoughts and peace will fill
your heart...Begin the day with joyful soul and joy will be your
part...Begin the day with friendliness, keep friendly all day long...
Keep in your soul a friendly thought, your heart a friendly song...
Have in your mind a world of cheer for all who come your way...
And they will bless you too, in turn, and wish you "Happy
Day!"...Begin each day with friendly thoughts and as the day goes
on...Keep friendly, loving, good and kind just as you were at
dawn..The day will be a friendly one and then at night you'll
find...That you were happy all day long through friendly thoughts
in mind.

Author Unknown

The love of friendship should be gratuitous.
You ought not to have or to love a friend for what he will give you.
If you love him for the reason that he will supply you with money
or some other temporal favor, you love the gift rather than him. A
friend should be loved freely for himself, and not for anything else.

St. Augustine

Four things are specially the property of friendship: love and affection, security and joy. And four things must be tried in friendship: faith, intention, discretion and patience. Indeed, as the sage says, all men would lead a happy life if only two tiny words were taken from them, mine and thine.

Aelred of Rievaulx

The glory of friendship is not the outstretched hand, nor the kindly smile, nor the joy of companionship; it is the spiritual inspiration that comes to one when he discovers that someone believes in him and is willing to trust him with his friendship.

Ralph Waldo Emerson

There is in friendship something of all relations, and something above them all. It is the golden thread that tied the hearts of all hearts of all the world.

John Evelyn

Life's Common Things

The things of every day are all so sweet—
The morning meadows wet with dew,
The dance of daisies in the noon;
The blue of far-off hills where twilight shadows lie;
The night, with all its tender mystery of sound
And silence, and God's starry sky!
Oh, life— the whole of life— is far too fleet.
The things of every day are all so sweet.

The common things of life are all so dear—
The waking in the warm half gloom
To find again the old familiar room,
The scents and sights and sounds that never tire;
The homely work, the plans, the lilt of baby's laugh,
The crackle of the open fire;
The waiting, then the footsteps coming near,
The opening door, your hand—clasp— and your kiss.
Is Heaven not after all the Now and Here?
The common things of life are all so dear.

Alice E. Allen

Friend

A warm handclasp,
A fond embrace,
A friendly smile
When face to face—
A cheerful greeting
Which seems to say
That you're concerned
This makes my day.

I sense a gladness
When we meet
Upon the stair
Or on the street.
Your sparkling eye—
This simple act
Makes glad my heart,
Now, that's a fact.

Louis Everett Downing

The Third Self of Friendship

"The meeting of two personalities is like the contact of two chemical substances; if there is any reaction, both are transformed."

Carl Jung

Friendship is a special kind of human experience.
One person might explain the special feeling by saying,
"We understand each other because we're on the same wave length." Another might say, "We are free to be ourselves with each other and don't have to worry about what people say."
A third: "Our friendship is like a protective cloud that surrounds us, and when we're together we feel safe, secure and trusting."
Or: "Whenever I'm with friends I'm open to new ideas and experiences and that is exciting." The secret of that fresh, alive, open and excited feeling seems to be that friendship provides a chance to live a new life. "Friendship is a second existence," explained Baltasar Gracian. People talk about friendship as if it has a life of its own: being born, growing, passing through crises, weakening and sometimes dying. Perhaps this way of talking about friendship provides the most fundamental insight of all— that friendship is a thing in itself, that is real, unique and personal. It can be called a third self, a new reality distinct from the friends themselves.

Muriel James and Louis Savary

A Time To Be Silent

There may be moments in friendship, as in love, when silence is beyond words. The faults of our friend may be clear to us, but it is well to seem to shut our eyes to them. Friendship is usually treated by the majority of mankind as a tough and everlasting thing which will survive all manner of bad treatment. But this is an exceedingly great and foolish error; it may die in an hour of a single unwise word; its conditions of existence are that it should be dealt with delicately and tenderly, being as it is a sensible plant and not a roadside thistle. We must not expect our friend to be above humanity.

Ouida

The Blessing of Friendship

A blessed thing it is for any man or woman to have a friend; one human soul whom we can trust utterly; who knows the best and the worst of us, and who loves us in spite of all our faults; who will speak the honest truth to us, while the world flatters us to our face, and laughs at us behind our back; who will give us counsel and reproof in the day of prosperity and self-conceit; but who, again, will comfort and encourage us in the day of difficulty and sorrow, when the world leaves us alone to fight our own battle as we can.

Charles Kingsley

No. 15

COLLECTED TREASURES

PAPILIO ULYSSES

Gift for a Friend

If, instead of a gem or even a flower, we could cast the gift of a lovely thought into the heart of a friend, that would be giving as angels give.

George MacDonald

Happiness

Man strives for glory, honor, fame,
That all the world may know his name.
Amasses wealth by brain and hand;
Becomes a power in the land,
But when he nears the end of life
And looks back over the years of strife,
He finds that happiness depends
On none of those but love of friends.

Author Unknown

We cannot tell the precise moment when friendship is formed. As in filling a vessel drop by drop, there is at last a drop which makes the heart run over.

James Boswell

Tribute to a Dear Friend

A real and dear friend
Is a rare, precious blend
Of rapport, understanding, and trust;
Who knows of our tears
And our joys through the years,
With whom all our plans are discussed;

Dear friends are those
Who never disclose
The dreams we entrust to their keeping;
They watch through the night
Till the morning's first light—
While others care not, and are sleeping.

Dear friends never change
We never feel strange
But always at home when they're near;
Friendships like these
Make fond memories
Which just grow increasingly dear;

Their worth can't be told
In silver or gold,
For love can't be measured on charts;
They've a most special place
Which time can't erase
In that one certain spot in our hearts!

Katherine Nelson Davis

Old Friendship

Beautiful and rich is an old friendship,
Grateful to the touch as ancient ivory,
Smooth as aged wine, or sheen of tapestry
Where light has lingered, intimate and long.
Full of tears and warm is an old friendship
That asks no longer deeds of gallantry,
Or any deed at all—
save that the friend shall be
Alive and breathing somewhere,
like a song.

Eunice Tietjens

A Friend Is...

A friend is someone who helps you clean up the dishes and you don't even have to protest once.

...that one word "hello" over the phone that can make you feel better than 10 minutes of conversation with anyone else.

...deep talks that go on until 3 a.m. On a work night!

A friend is more than a shoulder to cry on. A friend is the kind of understanding that makes crying unnecessary.

...someone to call in a hurry when something really watchable is on TV.

...sharing a pizza.

A friend is someone you can do nothing with and enjoy it.

...one good reason for believing in ESP.

...someone who won't say, "You look terrible!" when you look terrible.

A friend is the one who is already there doing it when everyone else is saying, "Is there anything I can do?"

...someone who will quietly destroy the snapshot that makes you look like the bride of Frankenstein.

...not too much sugar and just enough spice.

A friend is the kind of person who never wants to dress alike.

...someone who dislikes the same people you do.

...a little bit different every day but always the same.

A friend is someone who really is glad when you succeed.

...a believer in the spur of the moment.

...someone with whom you can either a borrower or a lender be.

A friend is a person who knows your sensitive spots but will never poke you there.

...a whole lot of wonderful people rolled into one.

...someone you can trade secrets with and never worry.

...laughter and going places and doing new things and having the best time ever.

A friend is the closest thing to me there is in more ways than one.

Gayle Lawrence

CAMELLIA

The first camellias were imported into *the most eighteenth century. They were brought over from China, Japan, Korea and Burma where they were growing wild.

The camelia flowers from late winter to spring

fig 16

JAPONICA

Because of a friend, life is a little stronger, fuller, more gracious thing for the friend's existence, whether he be near or far. If the friend is close at hand, that is best; but if he is far away he still is there to think of, to wonder about, to hear from, to write to, to share life and experience with, to serve, to honor, to admire, to love.

Arthur Christopher Benson

Friendship consists of forgetting what one gives, and remembering what one receives.

Alexandre Dumas

The most agreeable of all companions is a simple frank person, without any high pretensions to an oppressive greatness—one who loves life, and understands the use of it; obliging alike at all hours; above all, of a golden temper, and steadfast as an anchor. For such a one we gladly exchange the greatest genius, the most brilliant wit, the profoundest thinker.

Gotthold Ephraim Lessing

Happiness

Happiness is something more
Than what a man lays by in store,
More than prestige, more than power
Or fleeting pleasures of the hour.

Happiness is kindness living
In friendly hearts, in selfless giving,
A will to feel with one another
And treat a neighbor as a brother.

It is a faith, the nobler plan
That seeks the good in every man,
That leaves all censure unexpressed,
Forgives the flaw and sees the best!

Happiness is gold refined
Within the heart, a state of mind,
No need to travel, near or far,
You seek and find it—where you are!

A.G. Walton

God Give Me Joy

God give me joy in the common things:
In the dawn that lures, the eve that sings.

In the new grass sparkling after rain,
In the late winds wild and weird refrain;

In the springtime's spacious field of gold,
In the precious light by winter doled.

God give me joy in the love of friends,
In their dear home talk as summer ends;

In the songs of children, unrestrained;
In the sober wisdom age has gained.

God give me joy in the tasks that press,
In the memories that burn and bless;

In the thought that life has love to spend,
In the faith that God's at journey's end.

God give me hope for each day that springs
God give me joy in the common things!

Thomas Curtis Clark

Words from "The Prophet" on Friendship

And a youth said, Speak to us of Friendship.

And he answered, saying: Your friend is your needs answered.

He is your field which you sow with love and keep with thanksgiving.

And he is your board and your fireside.

For you come to him with your hunger, and you seek him for peace.

When your friend speaks his mind you fear not the "nay" in your own mind, nor do you withhold the "ay."

And when he is silent, your heart ceases not to listen to his heart;

For without words, in friendship, all thoughts, all desires, all expectations are born and shared, with joy that is unclaimed.

When you part from your friend, you grieve not;

For that which you love most in him may be clearer in his absence, as the mountain to the climber is clearer from the plain.

And let there be no purpose in friendship save the deepening of the spirit.

For love that seeks aught but the disclosure of its own mystery is not love but a net cast forth: and only the unprofitable is caught.

And let your best be for your friend.

If he must know the ebb of your tide, let him know its flood also.

For what is your friend that you should seek him with hours to kill?

Seek him always with hours to live.

For it is his to fill your need, but not your emptiness.

And in the sweetness of friendship let there be laughter, and sharing of pleasures.

For in the dew of little things the heart finds its morning and is refreshed.

Kahlil Gibran

Understanding and Trust

The very best thing is good talk, and the thing that helps it most is friendship. How it dissolves the barriers that divide us, and loosens all constraints, and diffuses itself like some fine old cordial through all the veins of life—this feeling that we understand and trust each other, and wish each other heartily well! Everything into which it really comes is good. It transforms letter writing from a task to a pleasure. It makes music a thousand times more sweet. The people who play and sing not at us, but to us—how delightful it is to listen to them! Yes, there is a talkability that can express itself even without words. There is an exchange of thoughts and feelings which is happily alike in speech and in silence. It is quietness pervaded with friendship.

Henry van Dyke

The Hours That Truly Count

Life may scatter us and keep us apart; it may prevent us from thinking very often of one another; but we know that our comrades are some-where "our there"—where, one can hardly say—silent, forgotten, but deeply faithful. And when our paths cross theirs, they greet us with such manifest joy, shake us so gaily by the shoulders! Indeed we are accustomed to waiting...We forget that there is no hope of joy except in human relations. If I summon up those memories that have left me with an enduring savor, if I draw up the balance sheet of the hours in my life that have truly counted, surely I find only those that no wealth could have procured me. True richness cannot be bought.

Antoine de Saint-Exupéry

Spring time tulips

gloria in excelsis deo

To Receive

It is more blessed to give than to receive...(But) the givers who can not take in return miss one of the finest graces in life, the grace of receiving...To receive gratefully from others is to enhance their sense of their worth. It puts them on a give-and-take level, the only level on which real fellowship can be sustained. It changes one of the ugliest things in the world, patronage, into one of the richest things in the world, friendship.

Halford E. Luccock

"Stay" is the most charming word in a friend's vocabulary.

Amos Bronson Alcott

Greater love hath no man than this,
that a man lay down his life for his friends.
Ye are my friends, if ye do whatsoever
I command you.
Henceforth I call you not servants;
for the servant knoweth not what his lord doeth;
but I have called you friends.
...Ye have not chosen me,
but I have chosen you.

John 15:13-16

What Is a Friend?

A friend is someone tried and true,
That you can tell your troubles to,
A gentle smile, a happy face
That makes the world a better place.
A friend is someone that is yours
As long as time and life endures,
Sharing cherished moments when
You know you never need pretend.

A friend is someone "fair and square"
Who comforts just by being there,
A fellow–traveler who brings
New meaning to the "little things."
Who always has the time to say
A word to brighten up your day,
Who helps you to accomplish more
Than you ever have done before.

A friend brings out the best you are,
Within the darkest night a star,
Throughout the greyest days a beam
Of sunlight stitched along each seam.

Who senses what you never say,
And somehow likes you just the way you are,
in spite of all you lack,
And each of us on looking back,
Recalls a voice, a special face
No other person can replace,
Who brushes back the doubt and care,
Just because he's always there!
A prize that each of us must earn,
Who helps us grow and helps us learn,
Asking nothing save a part
Of tenderness within our heart.

Because they are of such a kind,
A friend like this is hard to find.
I think by now we all have seen
That they are "few and far between."
Heaven's Emissary, he
Who leads us toward Eternity
Becoming a reflection of
God's deep and everlasting love.

                    Grace E. Easley

Friendship

There are marvelous joys in friendship. This is easily understood as soon as one realizes that joy is contagious. If my presence gives a friend some real happiness, the sight of his happiness is enough to make me in turn feel happy; thus the joy that each of us gives is returned to him; at the same time, vast reserves of joy are released; both friends say to themselves: "I had happiness in me that I wasn't making use of."

The source of happiness is within us, I'll admit that; and there is nothing sadder to see than people dissatisfied with themselves and with everything else, and who have to tickle each other in order to be able to laugh. However, it must be added that a happy man quickly forgets that he is happy once he is alone; all his joy soon becomes numbed; he sinks into a kind of unawareness bordering on stupor. An inner feeling needs an external form of manifestation. If some tyrant or other imprisoned me in order to teach me respect for the mighty, I would make it a rule of good health to laugh every day all alone; I would exercise my joy just as I would exercise my legs.

Here is a bundle of dry branches. They seem as inert as earth; if you leave them there, they will become earth. However, locked within them is a hidden ardor which they captured from the sun. Bring the smallest flame near them and soon you will have a crackling fire. All you had to do was rattle the door and awaken the prisoner.

In the same way, there must be a kind of starting signal to awaken joy. When a baby laughs for the first time, his laughter expresses nothing at all; he is not laughing because he is happy; instead I should say that he is happy because he is laughing; he enjoys laughing, just has he enjoys eating, but first he has to try eating. This is not only true for laughter; one needs words in order to know what one is thinking. As long as one is alone, one cannot be oneself. Simple-minded moralists say that loving means forgetting yourself; that is too simplistic; the more you get away from yourself, the more you are yourself; and the more you feel alive. Don't let your wood rot in the cellar.

Alain

Sharing the Good and the Bad

We may describe friendly feeling towards any one as wishing for him what you believe to be good things, not for your own sake but for his, and being inclined, so far as you can, to bring these things about. A friend is one who feels thus and excites these feelings in return: those who think they feel thus towards each other think themselves friends. This being assumed, it follows that your friend is the sort of man who shares your pleasure in what is good and your pain in what is unpleasant, for your sake and for no other reason. This pleasure and pain of his will be the token of his good wishes for you, since we all feel glad at getting what we wish for, and pained at getting what we do not. Those, then, are friends to whom the same things are good and evil.

Aristotle

To a Friend

Because you are my friend
I long today
To bring you some imperishable gift
Of beauty:

Something glowing and warm
Like the coals of living fire,
Something as cool and sweet
As blue lilies at dawn,
Something as restful and clean
As smooth white sheets at night
When one is very tired,
Something with the taste of spring water
From high places,
Or like the tang of cool purple grapes
To the mouth.

But O my friend,
Since I cannot buy such gifts for you,
Come go with me
Out into the little everyday fields of living,
And let us gather in our baskets, like manna,
God's gift to us;

The down-pouring, exquisite beauty
Of life itself!

Grace Noll Crowell

Friends Come, Friends Go

Friends come, friends go;
the loves men know are ever fleeting;
In song and smile a little while
we read their kindly greeting;
With warmth and cheer they linger near,
the friends we fondly treasure;
Then on a day they drift away,
a loss no words can measure.
This much we know: friends come, friends go,
as April's gladness passes,
As sun and shade, in swift parade,
paint changes on meadow grasses.
And though we grieve to see them leave,
in thought we still enfold them;
In Memory's Net we keep them yet,
and thus can ever hold them.
They come, they go—these Loves we know.
Life's Tides are ever moving;
But year on year, they still seem near—
so great the power of loving.

Author Unknown

What Is Life Without a Friend?

Say not that friendship's but a name,
Sincere we none can find;
An empty bubble in the air,
A phantom of the mind.
What is life without a friend?
A dreary race to run,
A desert where no water is,
A world without a sun.

Henry Alford

Arithmetic

Count your garden by the flowers,
Never by the leaves that fall;
Count your days by golden hours,
Don't remember clouds at all.
Count your nights by stars, not shadows,
Count your years with smiles, not tears,
Count your blessings, not your troubles,
Count your age by friends, not years.

Author Unknown

Friends Are Not a One-Way Street

A few weeks ago in New York an old and valued friend remarked, "I don't bother with anyone who bores me. I have cut down all my contacts to a minimum, I see only those people whom I really enjoy."

With the instantaneous reaction of the very busy I thought for a moment, how wonderful. To have matters so arranged that one would be spared the countless contacts that often seem frantically and futilely time-consuming.

And yet, on reflection, I'm not so sure.

Aren't friendships, on whatever level, a part of human fortune? Friendships can be infinitely varied. And by their very differentness the whole pattern of one's days can be enlivened, and in so many ways rewarding.

Sift through your friendships; sort them.

There is the rich inner circle of those people who are dearest to the heart. Usually these are the persons to whom we can most honestly express our deepest selves. And even though we may not see them for days, weeks on end—even years—the bond remains strong and special and true.

Yet would we not be the poorer without the infinite variety of others?

Friends can be friends for so many different reasons. There is the wonderfully helpful neighbor who is always willing to give you a hand with the children.

There is the witty one who can always make you laugh.

There is the one who sends over bones for the dog, and is generous with praise for your growing crew.

There is the quiet soul who occasionally comes up with a startling gem of philosophy.

It takes patience sometimes to appreciate the true values in the people with whom circumstances have surrounded us. It takes awareness to recognize these values when they appear.

Yet almost everyone has something uniquely his own to contribute to our lives—and equally important, a place in his own life that perhaps we alone can satisfy.

The heart has many doors. Don't be too quick to bolt them.

Marjorie Holmes

On the level of the human spirit an equal, a companion, an understanding heart is one who can share a man's point of view. What this means we all know. Friends, companions, lovers, are those who treat us in terms of our unlimited worth to ourselves. They are closest to us who best understand what life means to us, who feel for us as we feel for ourselves, who are bound to us in triumph and disaster, who break the spell of our loneliness.

Henry Alonzo Myers

Oh, the comfort; the inexpressible comfort of feeling safe with a person; having neither to weigh thoughts nor measure words, but to pour them all out, just as they are, chaff and grain together, knowing that a faithful hand will take and sift them, keep what is worth keeping and then, with the breath of kindness, blow the rest away.

Dinah Maria Mulock Craik

At eighteen, friendship is the buoyant acceptance of those who play and work and laugh and dream together. As a man gets older, he wants friends to stimulate him, to keep his mind active and young.

Bernhard Baruch

All Losses Restored

When to the sessions of sweet silent thought
I summon up remembrance of things past,
I sigh the lack of many a thing I sought,
And with old woes new wail my dear time's waste:
Then can I drown an eye, unused to flow,
For precious friends hid in death's dateless night,
And weep afresh love's long since cancell'd woe,
And moan the expense of many a vanish'd sight:
Then can I grieve at grievances foregone,
And heavily from woe to woe tell o'er
The sad account of fore-bemoaned moan,
Which I now pay as if not paid before.
But if the while I think on thee, dear friend,
All losses are restored and sorrows end.

William Shakespeare

There are three friendships which are advantageous, and three which are injurious... Friendship with the upright, with the sincere, and with the man of much observation, these are advantageous. Friendship with the man of specious airs, with the insinuatingly soft, and with the glib-tongued, these are injurious.

Confucius

A Friend

Crossing the uplands of time,
Skirting the borders of night,
Scaling the face of the peak of dreams,
We enter the region of light,
And hastening on with eager intent,
Arrive at the rainbow's end,
And here uncover the pot of gold
Buried deep in the heart of a friend.

Grace Goodhue Coolidge

Surrender to Time

It may seem, looking back, that becoming a friend... takes place in an instant. If we examine the experience, however, we discover that a long preparation through time precedes those moments which friends finally recognize and respond to each other. If we do not surrender to time, we may never recognize our true selves nor the true selves of others; we may not be able to enter those instants in which we see someone else in a way that no one else has ever seen them before...

Friends move toward each other through time. When they meet they are able to respond to all that they have come to recognize as valuable. Time is the tide that brings us together when we are ready for the challenge of friendship.

Eugene Kennedy

Special People

There are red-letter days in our lives when we meet people who thrill us like a fine poem, people whose handshake is brimful of unspoken sympathy and whose sweet, rich natures impart to our eager, impatient spirits a wonderful restfulness which is in its essence divine...

Perhaps we never saw them before and they may never cross our life's path again; but the influence of their calm, mellow natures is a libation poured upon our discontent, and we feel its healing touch as the ocean feels the mountain stream freshening its brine...

Helen Keller

That Good and Timely Deed

Friendships do not come by chance. Upon the looms of circumstance Fate weaves an intricate design—and threads of other lives entwine to make a pattern with our own. We were not made to walk alone. Our pathways lead to where we meet a friend in need. It seems that it was meant to be. And how important is that little touch of kindness at a time when it is needed most. These are kindnesses that you don't forget: The gesture of true sympathy that's made in all sincerity and comes when you are weary or upset. The understanding word that reaches down into your heart—at the very moment of your need. A well-timed act of friendliness that saves you from despair—even though it may be small. A good turn done for you that shows that someone has concern for you. How much it really means—that good and timely deed! The love that we appreciate is that which does not come too late to help us when we need it most of all!

Author Unknown

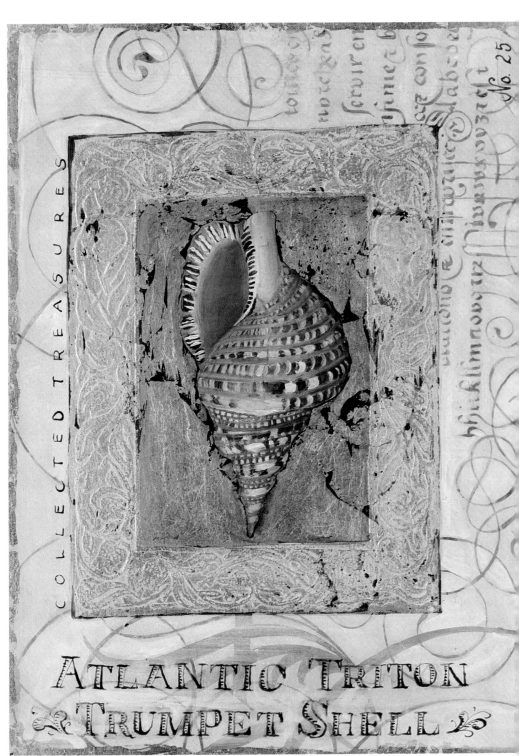

COLLECTED TREASURES

No. 25

ATLANTIC TRITON
TRUMPET SHELL

To My Friend

I ask but one thing of you, only one,

That always you will be my dream of you;

That never shall I wake to find untrue

All this I have believed and rested on,

Forever vanished, like a vision gone

Out into the night. Alas how few

There are who strike in us a chord we knew existed,

but so seldom heard its tone

We tremble at the half-forgotten sound.

The world is full of rude awakenings

And heaven-born castles shattered to the ground,

Yet still our human longing vainly clings

To a belief in beauty through all wrongs.

O stay your hand, and leave my heart its songs!

Amy Lowell

With My Love As of Old

The roads we chose diverged so little at the setting
out and seemed so nearly side by side!
A little while we spoke across the way, then waved our hands,
and then...
The hills between, life's other voices and the nights,
The silences...

Old friend, no new friend takes your place
With me as well
The hours and days flow by and lengthen into years,
But I do not forget. And not a thought that you have had of me—
Whether you wrote or spoke it, or, more like,
Just thought of me and let it go at that—
But it came winging through the silences!

Wherever you are, across the distance I give you my hand,
With my love as of old.

John Palmer Gavit

A Garland for Friendship

Friendship is a country,
Of the young and young–in–heart,
Made of morning's greetings,
A warm and lovely part
Of phone calls and cups of tea,
Of days of hope and caring,
Friendship is sturdy refuge,
Forgiveness and sweet sharing
Memories and happy times,
Picnics, fun together,
Count among life's garlands
Friends who make heart's weather.

Gladys McKee

Thanks are due to the following authors, publishers, publications and agents for permission to use the material indicated.

•CORNELL UNIVERSITY PRESS, for an excerpt from *Are Men Equal?* by Henry Alonzo Myers. Copyright © 1945 by Henry Alonzo Myers.

•DOUBLEDAY & COMPANY, INC., for "Life's Common Things" by Alice E. Allen from *Treasurehouse of Inspirational Poetry and Prose.* Edited by A.L. Alexander. Copyright © 1966 by A.L. Alexander.

•FAMILY ALBUM, for "What Is a Friend" by Grace E. Easley from *The Family Album,* 10 Star Edition. Copyright © 1975 by the Family Album.

•GOLDEN QUILL PRESS, for "Happiness" from *Lyrics for Living* by Alfred G. Walton. Copyright © 1963 by Alfred G. Walton.

•HARCOURT BRACE JOVANOVICH, INC., for an excerpt from *Wind, Sand and Stars* by Antoine de Saint-Exupery. Copyright © 1939 by Antoine de Saint-Exupery, renewed in 1967 by Lewis Galantiere.

•HARPER & ROW PUBLISHERS, INC., for "God Give Me Joy" by Thomas Curtis Clark from *1000 Quotable Poems.* Copyright © 1936 Harper & Row Publishers, Inc.; for "To a Friend" from *Some Brighter Dawn* by Grace Noll Crowell. Copyright © 1943 by Harper & Row Publishers, Inc.; for "Friends Are Like Flowers" from *Poems of Inspiration and Courage* by Grace Noll Crowell. Copyright © 1942 by Harper & Row Publishers, Inc., renewed 1970 by Reid Crowell; for an excerpt from *The Heart of Friendship* by Muriel James and Louis Savary. Copyright © 1976 by Collins Associates Publishing, Inc.